# ¡Vamos a Escuchar! 1

## A Listening Comprehension Course for Junior Certificate Spanish

Rosemary Graham B.A., M. Litt.

**FOLENS**

# Acknowledgements

The author wishes to thank the following: my editor, Priscilla O'Connor, and Margaret Burns and John O'Connor of Folens Publishers, for their support, my friend Yolanda Quintanilla Aparicio for her invaluable comments, speakers Sonia de Acuña Roldán, Inmaculada Alonso Fajardo, Montserrat Calvo Velo, Antonio Echvarria Suárez, Iñaki Hernández Lasa, Francisco Merino Alonso, Lidia Montero Ameneiro, Jaime Ortega Montero, Montserrat de Pablo, Cristina Rodríguez Guntín, Paulo Rodríguez Fernández, Begoña Serrano and Yolanda Quintanilla Aparicio, artist Aileen Caffrey for the delightful illustrations and Gary Dermody for the maps and grids, sound engineer Gar Duffy, Trend Studios and All Write Media. Finally, I would like to thank my husband Bernard and our daughter Cathy for all their support during the preparation of this course.

**Editor:** Priscilla O'Connor
**Design & Layout:** Karen Hoey
**Illustrations:** Aileen Caffrey, Gary Dermody

© Rosemary Graham 2009

Produced in Ireland by Folens Publishers, Hibernian Industrial Estate, Greenhills Road, Tallaght, Dublin 24

ISBN: 978-1-84741-241-6

The author and Publisher wish to acknowledge the following for permission to reproduce photographs:

Alamy Images, Getty Images, iStockphotos. Photo of Kilometro 0, Puerta del Sol, Madrid, by Håkan Svensson (http://upload.wikimedia.org/wikipedia/commons/7/76/MadridPuertaDelSol_Km0.jpg), licensed under Creative Commons Attribution 2.5 licence.

All rights reserved. No part of this publication may be reproduced or transmitted in any form or by any means (stencilling, photocopying, etc.) for whatever purpose, even purely educational, without written permission from the publisher.

The publisher reserves the right to change, without further notice at any time, the specification of this product, whether by change of materials, colours, bindings, format, text revision or any other characteristic.

# Contents

| | | |
|---|---|---|
| | Foreword............................................................ | vi |
| | To the student.................................................... | vii |
| Unit 1 | Un joven en Barcelona ....................................... | 1 |
| Unit 2 | De compras ......................................................... | 2 |
| Unit 3 | Fiestas en España ............................................... | 4 |
| Unit 4 | Una visita a España ............................................ | 5 |
| Unit 5 | ¿Qué te llevas cuando vas de viaje?................. | 6 |
| Unit 6 | ¿Dónde están? ..................................................... | 7 |
| Unit 7 | Al Prado ............................................................... | 8 |
| Unit 8 | Chateando ........................................................... | 9 |
| Unit 9 | En el bar ............................................................... | 10 |
| Unit 10 | Una encuesta sobre el ocio ............................... | 11 |
| Unit 11 | En un hotel .......................................................... | 12 |
| Unit 12 | Rutina diaria de Patricio y Josefa .................... | 13 |
| Unit 13 | Mis padres ........................................................... | 15 |
| Unit 14 | Pidiendo direcciones ......................................... | 16 |
| Unit 15 | ¡Buen viaje! .......................................................... | 17 |
| Unit 16 | El club de fútbol ................................................. | 18 |
| Unit 17 | Mi colegio ............................................................ | 19 |
| Unit 18 | La Sra. Ordóñez compra un regalo .................. | 21 |
| Unit 19 | ¿Qué te gusta más? ¿Qué te gusta menos?..... | 22 |
| Unit 20 | Amigos ................................................................. | 24 |
| Unit 21 | Conversación con una modelo famosa ........... | 26 |
| Unit 22 | ¿Dígame? .............................................................. | 27 |
| Unit 23 | Los sábados ......................................................... | 28 |
| Unit 24 | En la estación de trenes .................................... | 30 |
| Unit 25 | Así es mi vida ...................................................... | 31 |
| Unit 26 | Anuncios (1) ........................................................ | 32 |
| Unit 27 | ¿Qué tiempo hace? ............................................. | 33 |
| Unit 28 | Mari Carmen y Lucía en McDonald's ............... | 34 |

| | | |
|---|---|---|
| Unit 29 | ¿En qué sitio están? | 35 |
| Unit 30 | Buen Apetito | 36 |
| Unit 31 | El Parque de Atracciones | 37 |
| Unit 32 | Programas de televisión | 38 |
| Unit 33 | Una au pair en Irlanda | 40 |
| Unit 34 | Una cena especial | 42 |
| Unit 35 | Tres llamadas telefónicas | 43 |
| Unit 36 | ¡Vamos a la playa! | 44 |
| Unit 37 | Supersticiones | 45 |
| Unit 38 | Mi pueblo | 46 |
| Unit 39 | Pepe va de compras | 47 |
| Unit 40 | Un hotel en Málaga | 48 |
| Unit 41 | ¡Han empezado las rebajas! | 49 |
| Unit 42 | Noticias (1) | 50 |
| Unit 43 | Mi piso | 52 |
| Unit 44 | Mensajes telefónicos (1) | 53 |
| Unit 45 | Reservando un billete de avión | 54 |
| Unit 46 | ¿Dónde está? | 55 |
| Unit 47 | Anuncios (2) | 56 |
| Unit 48 | Una entrevista con un actor famoso | 57 |
| Unit 49 | ¿Qué país es? | 58 |
| Unit 50 | La Sra. Guzmán se encuentra mal | 59 |
| Unit 51 | ¡Vaya récord! | 60 |
| Unit 52 | El tiempo en Galicia | 62 |
| Unit 53 | Ayudando en casa | 63 |
| Unit 54 | ¿En qué puedo ayudarle? | 65 |
| Unit 55 | ¿A qué se dedica? | 66 |
| Unit 56 | En una boutique | 68 |
| Unit 57 | Mensajes telefónicos (2) | 69 |
| Unit 58 | Juana visita a una adivina | 70 |
| Unit 59 | Una estudiante nueva | 71 |

| Unit 60 | En una agencia de viajes | 72 |
| Unit 61 | El gazpacho andaluz | 73 |
| Unit 62 | En un pequeño hotel | 74 |
| Unit 63 | Mi día ideal | 75 |
| Unit 64 | En el restaurante | 76 |
| Unit 65 | En el aeropuerto de Dublín | 77 |
| Unit 66 | Por favor, ¿para ir a …? | 78 |
| Unit 67 | Número equivocado | 79 |
| Unit 68 | Juan tiene gripe | 80 |
| Unit 69 | Anuncios (3) | 81 |
| Unit 70 | YouTube | 82 |
| Unit 71 | En la oficina del Jefe de Estudios | 83 |
| Unit 72 | *Guía del Ocio* | 84 |
| Unit 73 | Una visita a Madrid: sábado | 85 |
| Unit 74 | Una visita a Madrid: domingo | 86 |
| Unit 75 | Un padre llama a su hija a Irlanda | 87 |
| Unit 76 | Noticias (2) | 88 |
| Unit 77 | Un turista busca información | 89 |
| Unit 78 | Pastel de chocolate | 90 |
| Unit 79 | Anuncios (4) | 91 |
| Unit 80 | Algunas estadísticas sobre Las Fallas | 92 |
| Unit 81 | Un albergue para jóvenes | 93 |
| Unit 82 | Manolito quiere más dinero | 94 |
| Unit 83 | Una mañana catastrófica | 95 |
| Unit 84 | Problemas | 96 |
| Unit 85 | Noticias (3) | 97 |
| Unit 86 | El tiempo para esta semana | 98 |
| Unit 87 | La Navidad se acerca | 100 |
| Unit 88 | Los Sanfermines | 101 |
| Unit 89 | Lidia pierde una bolsa | 103 |
| Unit 90 | En la clase | 104 |

# Foreword

This second edition of ¡Vamos a Escuchar! 1 includes new and revised material featuring contemporary topics and cultural references:

- Of the 90 units in this book, several are entirely new, while many others have been substantially revised and updated.
- New idioms and other vocabulary have been included to reflect current usage.
- The book reflects the widespread use of modern communications technologies such as mobile phones, iPods, WiFi, the Internet, satellite TV, etc.
- The information provided in the units has been carefully researched to ensure that it is accurate and up-to-date, e.g. the phone numbering system in Spain, flight arrival times and flight numbers, statistics and dates.
- Students are encouraged to develop an interest in modern Spanish culture through references to television programmes, food, festivals and many other topics.

The main aim of language acquisition is communication and the listening skill is a fundamental part of this interaction. ¡Vamos a Escuchar! 1 is designed to help students practise aural skills in Spanish from elementary to intermediate level. ¡Vamos a Escuchar! 1 consists of two CDs containing 90 units of recorded material of approximately two hours' duration, a teacher's booklet containing the CD script and a student's exercise book of comprehension questions based on the units. It is suitable both for students in a classroom situation and for the student learning independently.

¡Vamos a Escuchar! 1 reflects closely the Junior Certificate aural examination syllabus and contains a wide variety of text types including dialogues, news items, weather forecasts, texts of factual/cultural interest, interviews, monologues, phone calls, phone messages, advertisements and announcements. Students are thus exposed to a wide variety of language situations and registers typically encountered in a Spanish-speaking environment. The units are carefully graded to present and reinforce key aspects of language appropriate to this level. Special attention is given to areas typically causing difficulty, such as *gustar*, *ser/estar*, *haber*, *tener* idioms, verb form and number.

The comprehension questions cater for students of varying abilities, and include direct questions, true/false statements, multiple-choice questions and completion of simple maps and grids.

The pace of the recordings is graduated and leads to that typically used in the Junior Certificate aural examination. In total, 13 native Spanish speakers from many areas took part in the recordings, thus giving the learner exposure to a wide variety of accents.

The Junior Certificate examination places heavy emphasis on the aural skill, an indication of its importance in language acquisition. ¡Vamos a Escuchar! 1 provides an opportunity for extensive practice in this area.

# To the student

The early stages of understanding the spoken word in a foreign language are the most difficult. However, the feeling of satisfaction and achievement as you begin to improve is well worth the patience and perseverance it takes.

When you have done, perhaps, one-third of this course, it might be an interesting exercise to listen again to the first few recordings. Without realising it, you have probably sharpened your listening skills considerably in the meantime, and therefore may well find the earlier texts relatively easy second time around.

And so it continues. As you reach new hurdles, the old ones begin to disappear. This is progress. ¡Ánimo y adelante!

## A Note on CD Track Numbering

Two CDs are supplied in this book. CD 1 covers Units 1–45, and CD 2 covers Units 46–90. Each unit or subunit has a corresponding CD track number, which is represented by a colour-coded icon, blue for CD 1 and red for CD 2.

For example:  means CD 1, track 2;

 means CD 2, track 12.

*To Bernard*

¡Vamos a escuchar! 1

# 1. Un joven en Barcelona

**Antonio introduces himself.**

🔵 2

1. What age is Antonio? .................................................
2. Where does he live? ..................................................
3. He has two sisters and one brother.  True ☐   False ☐
4. Where is the bank where he works situated? ...................
5. What are the opening hours of the bank? .......................
6. What is the advantage of travelling by metro, according to Antonio?
   ..........................................................................
7. What two disadvantages are there? .............................
   ..........................................................................
8. Name three things he does after work.
   (i) .....................................................................
   (ii) ....................................................................
   (iii) ...................................................................
9. Who is Pepita? ......................................................
10. What is she like? ..................................................

¡Vamos a escuchar! 1

## 2. De compras

**La Sra. González has a busy afternoon shopping.**

1. La Sra. González buys seven items in the first shop. Give details of the items and their weight or quantity.

    (i) ..................................................................................................
    (ii) .................................................................................................
    (iii) ................................................................................................
    (iv) ................................................................................................
    (v) .................................................................................................
    (vi) ................................................................................................
    (vii) ...............................................................................................

* * *

## ¡Vamos a escuchar! 1

**4**

**2.** The magazine she buys for herself is about:

fashion and beauty ☐   the home and garden ☐   entertainment ☐

**3.** What type of magazine does she buy for her husband?

...................................................................................................

**4.** What else does she buy in the same place? ........................................

* * *

**5**

**5.** What does she try to buy in the next shop? ........................................

**6.** What date does the shopkeeper tell her it is? ....................................

**7.** Where does she say she will try to buy the item? ..............................

...................................................................................................

¡Vamos a escuchar! 1

## 3. Fiestas en España

You will hear the dates of some local and national holidays in Spain. Fill in the dates that you hear. In some cases there is more than one holiday in the same month. The dates are not presented in the same order as the grid. The first one is done for you.

◯ 6

| MONTH | DAY(S) | | |
|---|---|---|---|
| January | | | |
| February | | | |
| March | | | |
| April | | | |
| May | | | |
| June | | | |
| July | | | |
| August | 15 | | |
| September | | | |
| October | | | |
| November | | | |
| December | | | |

¡Vamos a escuchar! 1

# 4. Una visita a España

**Anna is visiting Spain for the first time.**

🔵 7

1. Anna is Dutch.       True ☐       False ☐
2. She is visiting Spain in:  spring ☐   summer ☐   autumn ☐   winter ☐
3. For how long is she staying in Spain? ..................................................
4. In which city is she staying? ..................................................
5. What is the first thing she notices when she arrives?
   ..................................................................................................

6. The Torres family:
   (a)  go to the football stadium a lot.
   (b)  watch football regularly on TV.
   (c)  live near a football stadium.

   Put the correct letter in the box. ☐

7. Anna finds three things different from her native country. What are they?
   ..................................................................................................
   ..................................................................................................

8. During the first few days, Anna can only say:
   ..................................................................................................

9. What does she hope to do? ..................................................

¡Vamos a escuchar! 1

## 5. ¿Qué te llevas cuando vas de viaje?

**Four people say what they pack when they go on a trip. What items do they bring?**

🔘 8
1. Speaker 1

   (i) ........................ (ii) ........................ (iii) ............................

   (iv) ........................ (v) ............................

🔘 9
2. Speaker 2

   (i) ........................ (ii) ........................ (iii) ............................

   (iv) ........................ (v) ............................

🔘 10
3. Speaker 3

   (i) ........................ (ii) ........................ (iii) ............................

   (iv) ........................ (v) ............................

🔘 11
4. Speaker 4

   (i) ........................ (ii) ........................ (iii) ............................

   (iv) ........................ (v) ............................

## 6. ¿Dónde están?

You will hear four short dialogues. Can you guess where they take place?

🔘 12
1. ........................................................................................

🔘 13
2. ........................................................................................

🔘 14
3. ........................................................................................

🔘 15
4. ........................................................................................

¡Vamos a escuchar! 1

# 7. Al Prado

**Someone is looking for directions to the Prado art gallery.**

1. Where exactly is the bus stop for the Prado?
   ..................................................................................

2. How often does a bus pass? ........................................................

3. How long does the bus journey take? ........................................

4. What information makes the man feel annoyed?
   ..................................................................................

¡Vamos a escuchar! 1

## 8. Chateando

Four young people join an Internet chatroom. Fill in the information which they give about themselves.

🔵 17–20

|  | **PEDRO** | **LAURA** | **DIEGO** | **CONCHA** |
|---|---|---|---|---|
| Native city |  |  |  |  |
| Age |  |  |  |  |
| Colour of hair |  |  |  |  |
| Colour of eyes |  |  |  |  |
| Personality |  |  |  |  |
| Pastime(s) |  |  |  |  |
| Career hopes |  |  |  |  |
| Favourite possession |  |  |  |  |

¡Vamos a escuchar! 1

## 9. En el bar

**A man orders some food and drink for his family in the local bar.**

🔘 21

1. What beverages does the man order? .................................................
   ....................................................................................

2. Why does he decide to sit outside?
   ....................................................................................

3. Besides Spanish omelette, which of the following snacks does the bar attendant mention?

   meatballs ☐    anchovies ☐    olives ☐    Russian salad ☐
   salad ☐        croquettes ☐   prawns ☐    almonds ☐

4. The man wants the Spanish omelette served:

   hot ☐            cold ☐

5. What else does the man ask for? ........................................................

¡Vamos a escuchar! 1

# 10. Una encuesta sobre el ocio

You will hear the results of a survey which was carried out to find out what young people in their local area do in their leisure time. Fill in the results of the survey.

| NUMBER DOING ACTIVITY | ACTIVITY |
|---|---|
|  | Play guitar |
|  |  |
|  | Read gossip magazines |
|  |  |
|  | Go jogging |
|  |  |
| 10 |  |
|  |  |
|  | Listen to music on their iPod |
|  |  |
|  |  |

¡Vamos a escuchar! 1

# 11. En un hotel

**A man is booking a hotel room.**

🔵 23

1. The man is booking:

   (a)  a single room ☐          a double room ☐

   (b)  with a bathroom ☐        without a bathroom ☐

   (c)  for Monday ☐             Tuesday ☐
        Wednesday ☐              Thursday ☐
        Friday ☐

2. How much is the room per night?

   ..................................................................................................................

3. What facilities does the room provide?

   ..................................................................................................................

   ..................................................................................................................

4. Breakfast is served between ........................... and ........................

5. What two things does the receptionist ask him for?

   (i) ...............................................................................................................

   (ii) ..............................................................................................................

6. What is the number of his bedroom? ....................................................

7. What can be seen from his balcony? ...................................................

8. Where is the lift situated? ...................................................................

## 12. Rutina diaria de Patricio y Josefa

You will hear Patricio's morning routine and Josefa's afternoon/evening routine. Fill in the missing information in the grids.

### Patricio's routine

| TIME | ACTION |
|---|---|
| 7.15 | |
| | |
| | Gets dressed |
| | |
| | |
| | |
| 9.00 | |
| | |
| | |

## Josefa's routine

| TIME | ACTION |
|---|---|
| 1.30 | |
| | |
| | |
| | Has an afternoon snack |
| | |
| | |
| | |
| | |

¡Vamos a escuchar! 1

# 13. Mis padres

**Rosario describes her parents.**

🔘 26

1. What age is Rosario's mother? ...............................................
2. What does she look like? ...............................................
3. What two qualities does Rosario particularly mention that her mother has?
   (i) ...............................................
   (ii) ...............................................
4. What two things put her mother in a bad mood?
   (i) ...............................................
   (ii) ...............................................

\* \* \*

🔘 27

5. How old is Rosario's father? ...............................................
6. What part of Spain does he come from? ...............................................
7. What does he look like? ...............................................
8. What does he not like doing? ...............................................
9. Where does he go on Saturday evenings? ...............................................
10. What does he do there? ...............................................
    ...............................................

¡Vamos a escuchar! 1

## 14. Pidiendo direcciones

Three people are looking for directions. In each case, X marks the spot where the speaker is. Write down A, B and C, to indicate the position of:

 28–30

   (a)   the post office.

   (b)   the swimming pool.

   (c)   the Banco de España.

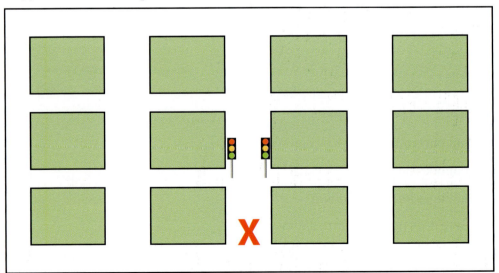

¡Vamos a escuchar! 1

# 15. ¡Buen viaje!

Four school friends talk about their summer holiday plans. Fill in the details.

🔊 31–34

| | | | | |
|---|---|---|---|---|
| **HOLIDAY DESTINATION** | | | | |
| **MEANS OF TRANSPORT** | | | | |
| **GOING WITH WHOM** | | | | |
| **DURATION OF HOLIDAY** | | | | |
| **PLANS WHILE ON HOLIDAY** | | | | |

¡Vamos a escuchar! 1

# 16. El club de fútbol

Francisco wants to join a football club and talks to the manager. Listen to their conversation and fill in the details below.

 35

Name      Francisco Domínguez

Age .................................................................................................

Date of birthday ................................................................................

Address .............................................................................................

............................................................................................................

Mobile telephone number ................................................................

How long playing football ................................................................

Preferred playing position ................................................................

Training days are ........................... and ...........................

Training times are      from ........................ to ...........................

                          and from ........................ to ...........................

¡Vamos a escuchar! 1

# 17. Mi colegio

**Nuria talks about her school.**

🔵 36

1. Where exactly is Nuria's school situated? ............................................
   ........................................................................

2. Approximately how many pupils are there in the school? ....................

3. Which of the following places does Nuria mention? Tick the correct boxes.

   | library | ☐ | bookshop | ☐ | gymnasium | ☐ |
   |---|---|---|---|---|---|
   | swimming-pool | ☐ | laboratory | ☐ | classrooms | ☐ |
   | canteen | ☐ | kitchen | ☐ | computer room | ☐ |
   | teachers' room | ☐ | shop | ☐ | office of Head of Studies | ☐ |

4. What two areas in the school grounds does Nuria mention?
   ........................................................................

5. Describe her uniform. ..........................................................
   ........................................................................
   ........................................................................

6. What does she wear when practising sports? ..................................
   ........................................................................

7. Why does she like having a uniform? .........................................
   ........................................................................

¡Vamos a escuchar! 1

8. What languages are studied in her school? ..........................................
   ..................................................................................................
9. What other subjects does Nuria mention? .........................................
   ..................................................................................................
10. Classes begin at ............................ and finish at ............................
11. Why does she prefer this timetable to that of some other schools?
    ..................................................................................................
12. Why does she like her school a lot? ................................................
    ..................................................................................................

¡Vamos a escuchar! 1

# 18. La Sra. Ordóñez compra un regalo

**La Sra. Ordóñez goes shopping for a present.**

🔘 37

1. What item of clothing does the woman want to buy? ..............................
2. For whom is she buying it and why? ...............................................
   ..............................................................................
3. What colour does she want? ........................................................
4. What size is she looking for? ......................................................
5. What pattern does the garment have? ............................................
6. What is the price of the garment? .................................................
7. The woman thinks it is a little expensive.   True ☐     False ☐
8. On what conditions can the garment be returned? ..............................
   ..............................................................................
9. How much change does the woman get? ..........................................

¡Vamos a escuchar! 1

# 19. ¿Qué te gusta más? ¿Qué te gusta menos?

You will hear three people talking about their likes and dislikes. First listen to what they like, and then fill in the details below.

**38**

Merche likes        (i) ............................... (ii) ...................................

                    (iii) ............................. (iv) ...................................

* * *

**39**

Manolo likes        (i) ............................... (ii) ...................................

                    (iii) ............................. (iv) ...................................

* * *

**40**

Alicia likes        (i) ............................... (ii) ...................................

                    (iii) ............................. (iv) ...................................

¡Vamos a escuchar! 1

**Now you will hear what they don't like. Fill in the details below.**

🔵 41

Merche dislikes  (i) .............................. (ii) ..............................
              (iii) .............................. (iv) ..............................

* * *

🔵 42

Manolo dislikes  (i) .............................. (ii) ..............................
              (iii) .............................. (iv) ..............................

* * *

🔵 43

Alicia dislikes  (i) .............................. (ii) ..............................
              (iii) .............................. (iv) ..............................

¡Vamos a escuchar! 1

## 20. Amigos

**Javi and Clara each talk about their best friend.**
🔘 44

### Javi

1. Describe Javi's friend, Pablo. ..............................................................
   ..............................................................................................
2. What age are Javi and his friend? ........................................................
3. Why do they know each other all their lives? ..........................................
   ..............................................................................................
4. In what way do they have similar personalities? ......................................
   ..............................................................................................
5. What interests do they share in common? ..............................................
   ..............................................................................................

* * *

¡Vamos a escuchar! 1

### Clara

🔘 45

**6.** How long have Clara and Bea known each other? ..................................

**7.** In what way are their family circumstances similar?

(i) ................................... (ii) ...................................

**8.** In what way do they have similar personalities? ..................................
...................................................................................

**9.** What interests do they have in common? ..................................
...................................................................................

**10.** Describe what Bea looks like. ..................................
...................................................................................

**11.** Describe Clara. ..................................
...................................................................................

## 21. Conversación con una modelo famosa

**A top model reveals some of the secrets of her good looks and fitness.**

◉ 46

1. The model never drinks alcohol or smokes.   True ☐   False ☐
2. What does she do to stay physically fit? ..................................................
   ..................................................................................................
3. What foods does she eat a lot? ..........................................................
4. What food does she limit? ................................................................
5. What kind of food does she not eat at all? ..........................................
6. How much water does she drink daily? ..............................................
7. How many hours' sleep does she try to get? ......................................
8. What weakness does she have regarding this regime?
   ..................................................................................................
9. What is her view on cosmetic surgery? ..............................................

¡Vamos a escuchar! 1

# 22. ¿Dígame?

**You will hear some snatches of three telephone conversations. Listen carefully and answer the questions below.**

**47**

1. What flight number is this person enquiring about? ..............................
2. At what time is the flight arriving? ..............................................
3. By how long is the flight delayed? ...............................................

\* \* \*

**48**

4. Paco says St Valentine's Day is on Saturday.  True ☐    False ☐

5. Paco and his girlfriend plan:

   (a) a romantic trip      (b) to see a romantic film      (c) a romantic meal out

   Put the correct letter in the box. ☐

\* \* \*

**49**

6. For what dates does this person wish to book a hotel bedroom?

   ............................................................................................

7. Why is there a problem with the booking? .........................................

   ............................................................................................

¡Vamos a escuchar! 1

# 23. Los sábados

**Some people talk about what they do on Saturdays.**
🔵 50

1. Until what time does this boy like to stay in bed on Saturdays? .....................
2. Where does he go when he gets up? .....................
3. What does he do there? .....................
   .....................

\* \* \*

🔵 51

4. What homework subjects does this girl do on Saturday morning?
   .....................

5. To what two places does she like to go in the afternoon?
   (i) ..................... (ii) .....................

\* \* \*

🔵 52

6. What must this person do in the morning? .....................
7. What might he do in the afternoon?
   (i) ..................... (ii) .....................
   (iii) .....................

\* \* \*

8. This girl works in a café from ........................... to ...........................
9. What does she do in her job? ......................................................
10. Describe what she wears at work. ................................................
11. Why does she like her job? .........................................................
   .........................................................................................

¡Vamos a escuchar! 1

## 24. En la estación de trenes

**Someone is buying train tickets to Seville.**

🔵 54

1. How many tickets is the woman buying? ............................................

2. They are:   single ☐      return ☐

3. On what basis is there a discount? ............................................
   ............................................

4. When does the next train leave? ............................................

5. At what time does the train arrive in Seville? ............................................

6. From what platform does it leave? ............................................

7. Passengers can get refreshments on the train.    True ☐     False ☐

8. Before getting on the train, the woman wants to buy:

   sweets ☐        a magazine ☐         a newspaper ☐

9. Where is the kiosk? ............................................

¡Vamos a escuchar! 1

# 25. Así es mi vida

**Mario describes his life**.

🔵 55

1. In what province does Mario live? ................................................
2. His village has 500 inhabitants.   True ☐      False ☐
3. How many brothers and sisters does he have? ........................
4. What products does his father grow? ......................................
5. On what day does his mother go to the market? ....................
6. She goes to the market:

    (a) to do her shopping    (b) to sell the products that they grow.

    Write the correct letter in the box. ☐
7. To what four countries does his father export?

    (i) ....................................... (ii) ...........................................

    (iii) ..................................... (iv) ...........................................
8. What activities does Mario enjoy with his cousins? ..................

    ...................................................................................................
9. Mario says his best friend is ...................................................
10. Why does Mario not want to be a farmer? ...............................

    ...................................................................................................

¡Vamos a escuchar! 1

# 26. Anuncios (1)

**You will hear some announcements. Listen carefully, and answer the questions below.**

🔵 56

1. What product is on offer? ....................................................................
2. What are the terms of the offer? ..........................................................
   ..............................................................................................

\* \* \*

🔵 57

3. When is the train leaving? ..................................................................
4. From what platform is it leaving? .......................................................

\* \* \*

🔵 58

5. What age is Ana? ..............................................................................
6. What is she wearing? ........................................................................
7. What is her hair like? ........................................................................
8. Where should she be brought, if she is found? ....................................

\* \* \*

🔵 59

9. Jordi is:    (a) a singer    (b) a dancer    (c) a musician

   Write the correct letter in the box. ☐

10. Where will the cabaret take place? ....................................................
11. At what time will the show start and finish? .......................................

¡Vamos a escuchar! 1

## 27. ¿Qué tiempo hace?

You will hear what the weather is like in various parts of Spain. Complete the grid. The first one is done for you.

🔵 60

| WHAT'S THE WEATHER LIKE? | WHERE? |
|---|---|
| It's showery. | Galicia |
|  |  |
|  |  |
|  |  |
|  |  |
|  |  |
|  |  |
|  |  |
|  |  |
|  |  |

¡Vamos a escuchar! 1

# 28. Mari Carmen y Lucía en McDonald's

**Lucía has decided to start a diet.**

🔘 61

1. What does Mari Carmen want to order for herself? ...............................
   ..................................................................
2. What does Lucía want to order, initially? ...........................................
3. How much weight does she want to lose? .......................................
4. What does her diet consist of? ..................................................
   ..................................................................
5. How long does the diet last? ....................................................
6. What does Mari Carmen offer to give her friend? .................................
   ..................................................................
7. Specify the order the two friends finally decide on. ...............................
   ..................................................................

¡Vamos a escuchar! 1

## 29. ¿En qué sitio están?

**You will hear four snatches of conversation.**

🎧 62

1. Where do you think this man is? .................................................
2. Give details of what he wishes to do. ............................................

* * *

🎧 63

3. Where do you think this girl is? ..................................................
4. What does the official ask her to do? ...........................................

* * *

🎧 64

5. Where do you think this woman is? .............................................
6. What three things does she ask the attendant to do? ..................
..................................................................................................

* * *

🎧 65

7. Where do you think this man is? ................................................
8. What exactly does he book? .....................................................
9. What does the girl ask him for? ................................................
10. What does she give the man? ..................................................

¡Vamos a escuchar! 1

# 30. Buen Apetito

**You will hear an advertisement promoting the Buen Apetito restaurant.**
🔊 66

1. Where is the restaurant situated? ..................................................................
2. How many years' experience do the restaurant owners have? .....................
3. They specialise in traditional food from ........................................................
4. For what occasions do they prepare a special menu?

    (i) ........................................ (ii) ............................................
    
    (iii) ........................................ (iv) ............................................

5. They are open:   from ........................ to ........................
   
     and from ........................ to ........................

6. On what day does the restaurant not open? ..................................................
7. Their email address is ...................................................................................
8. Their phone number is ..................................................................................

¡Vamos a escuchar! 1

# 31. El Parque de Atracciones

**Federico stops a woman in the street to ask about the theme park.**

 67

1. The woman gives Federico the numbers of two bus lines. What are they?

    (i) ……………………………… (ii) ……………………………………

2. What are the opening and closing times of the theme park: (a) on Fridays and (b) on Saturdays?

    (a) from……………………………… to………………………………………

    (b) from ……………………………… to………………………………………

3. Why does the woman know so much about the theme park? …………………

    ……………………………………………………………………………………

¡Vamos a escuchar! 1

## 32. Programas de televisión

**Four young people talk about television programmes.**

🔵 68

1. What kinds of films does this girl like to watch on television?
   .................................................................................................

2. What criticism does she have regarding the films shown on television?
   .................................................................................................

* * *

🔵 69

3. What sports does this person watch on television?
   (i) ............................ (ii) ............................ (iii) ............................
   (iv) ............................ (v) ............................

4. What kinds of television programmes does his sister like?
   .................................................................................................

* * *

### ¡Vamos a escuchar! 1

🔘 70

**5.** When does this girl particularly like watching television?
...................................................................................................

**6.** What does the programme that she likes include? ...........................
...................................................................................................

\* \* \*

🔘 71

**7.** Besides reality shows, this young man likes:

soap operas ☐   nature programmes ☐
competitions ☐   cooking programmes ☐

Tick the correct box.

**8.** What is the opinion of his parents on the programmes he watches?
...................................................................................................

**9.** What kinds of programmes do his parents watch?
...................................................................................................

**10.** What is his view of the programmes his parents watch? ...................
...................................................................................................

¡Vamos a escuchar! 1

## 33. Una au pair en Irlanda

**Paloma describes her life as an au pair with a family in Galway.**

🔵 72

1. What is the father's occupation? ..................................................
2. What is the mother's occupation? ..................................................
3. What age are the two children? ..................................................
4. Tick where appropriate:

   Paloma gets up at 7.30. ☐

   She takes a bath. ☐

   She organises the children. ☐

   She has toast, marmalade and coffee. ☐

   She brings the children to school. ☐

5. How long does it take to get to the school on foot? ..................................

¡Vamos a escuchar! 1

6. What four things does Paloma do in the morning to help?

   (i) ......................................... (ii) .........................................

   (iii) ....................................... (iv) .........................................

7. At what time does she collect the children from school? ..........................

8. What does she do when they return? ................................................
   ...............................................................................................

9. From what time is she free during the week? ......................................

10. She goes to evening classes on Tuesdays and Thursdays.   True ☐   False ☐

11. The classes start at ............................. and finish at ..........................

12. Why does she like meeting other au pairs? ........................................
    ...............................................................................................

13. What activities might she do at the weekend? ....................................
    ...............................................................................................

14. What is the only thing she does not like about Ireland?
    ...............................................................................................

¡Vamos a escuchar! 1

## 34. Una cena especial

**A restaurant table is being booked.**

🔘 73

1. For how many people is the table being booked? ......................................

2. For what time is it being booked? ......................................

3. What is the caller's name? ......................................

4. The receptionist asks the caller to spell his name because:

   (a) she has never heard the name before.

   (b) she has poor hearing.

   (c) the line is bad.

   (d) she has poor spelling.

   Write the correct letter in the box. ☐

5. What does the caller ask to be brought to the table?

   ......................................................................................................

6. What reason does he give for this request? ......................................

   ......................................................................................................

¡Vamos a escuchar! 1

## 35. Tres llamadas telefónicas

**Paula Machado is at home when three people telephone.**

🔘 74

1. When is Paula's mother coming back? .................................................
2. Who wishes to speak to Paula's mother? ............................................
3. What message does he leave for Paula's mother? ...............................
   ..........................................................................................................

\* \* \*

🔘 75

4. Who is the second person who phones Paula? ...................................
5. Where has Paula's mother gone? .......................................................
6. What does the caller tell Paula? ..........................................................

\* \* \*

🔘 76

7. What problem does Paula's friend Clara have? ...................................
   ..........................................................................................................
8. What favour does she ask of Paula? ..................................................

¡Vamos a escuchar! 1

## 36. ¡Vamos a la playa!

**Two friends decide to go to the beach.**

🔵 77

1. When and at what time do the girls plan to go to the beach?
   ....................................................................................................................
2. Why do they decide not to eat in a restaurant? ........................................
   ....................................................................................................................
3. What food and drink do they arrange to bring? ......................................
   ....................................................................................................................
4. Why do they decide not to bring the car? ................................................
   ....................................................................................................................
5. What is the number of the bus which goes to the beach? ...................
6. How often does it pass the Plaza Mayor? ................................................
7. Where in the Plaza Mayor do they arrange to meet? ...........................
   ....................................................................................................................

¡Vamos a escuchar! 1

# 37. Supersticiones

**Four people talk about superstitions.**

🔘 78
1. What day and date does this girl not like? ................................................
2. What does she not like to do on that particular day? ................................

\* \* \*

🔘 79
3. Which of this boy's relatives is superstitious? ...........................................
4. What colour does his relative not like? ....................................................
5. What does his relative always do in the morning? ....................................
...................................................................................................

\* \* \*

🔘 80
6. What does this man's mother not like to see? ..........................................
7. If a fly lands on his mother's nose, what does his mother believe will happen?
...................................................................................................

\* \* \*

🔘 81
8. Which of this girl's relatives is superstitious? ............................................
9. What two things does the relative not like to see? ...................................
...................................................................................................

45

¡Vamos a escuchar! 1

## 38. Mi pueblo

**Fátima describes her home town.**

🔊 82

1. Where is this town situated? ....................................................
2. How many inhabitants does it have? ..........................................
3. Eight shops are mentioned in the town square. What are they?

   (i) ........................ (ii) ........................ (iii) ........................
   (iv) ........................ (v) ........................ (vi) ........................
   (vii) ........................ (viii) ........................
4. Where does Fátima's father work? ...............................................
5. Who was Rosalía de Castro? ......................................................
6. Beside shops, what facilities does the town offer? ...........................
   .................................................................................................
7. What three facilities does the town not have?

   (i) ........................ (ii) ........................ (iii) ........................
8. Why does Fátima not like the close-knit community life of her town?
   .................................................................................................

¡Vamos a escuchar! 1

# 39. Pepe va de compras

**Pepe shops for clothes and gets a shock!**

🔘 83

1. What colour does the shop assistant say is in fashion this year? ....................

2. Fill in Pepe's size in these items of clothing.

   | Shirt |  |
   |---|---|
   | Trousers |  |
   | Jacket |  |

3. The brand of trousers which the shop assistant recommends is:

   French ☐    German ☐    Italian ☐

4. The trousers which the assistant shows Pepe cost ........................... euro.

5. What price is the shirt? ........................................................

6. What time does the shop assistant say it is? ...................................

47

¡Vamos a escuchar! 1

## 40. Un hotel en Málaga

**A hotel is being advertised.**

🔊 84

1. How far is the hotel from (a) Málaga and (b) the beach?

   (a) .................................... (b) ..............................................

2. How many bedrooms does it have? ..............................................

3. What do all the bedrooms have? ................................................
   ............................................................................................

4. What kind of food does the restaurant specialise in? .....................

5. Tick which of the following amenities the hotel also offers:

   | a jacuzzi ☐ | a TV room ☐ | a hairdresser's ☐ |
   | shops ☐ | tennis courts ☐ | a café bar ☐ |
   | a gym ☐ | a swimming pool ☐ | parking ☐ |
   | minigolf ☐ | a conference room ☐ | cabaret ☐ |

6. What is the telephone number of the hotel? ..................................

¡Vamos a escuchar! 1

## 41. ¡Han empezado las rebajas!

**Montse and Ana arrange to go shopping.**

🔊 85

1. Which of Ana's relatives is getting married and when? ...................................
   ................................................................................................................
2. Besides a dress, what would Ana like to buy for the wedding? ......................
3. By how much are the floral dresses reduced in Zara? ...............................
4. Her friend Montse would like to buy:
   (i) ........................... (ii) ............................ (iii) ...........................
   (iv) ........................... (v) ............................
5. Where and when do they arrange to meet? ..............................................
   ................................................................................................................

¡Vamos a escuchar! 1

# 42. Noticias (1)

**You will hear three news items.**

🔵 86

1. How many people died in this plane accident? ........................................
2. How many people were injured? ........................................
3. Where did the accident happen? ........................................
4. Who are among those who died? ........................................
5. How many people were on board approximately? ........................................
6. What is believed to have been the cause of the accident? ........................................

\* \* \*

🔵 87

7. This robbery took place:

   (a) in a savings bank.

   (b) in a boutique.

   (c) in a petrol station.

   (d) in a jeweller's.

   Write the correct letter in the box. ☐

8. How many robbers were involved? ........................................
9. At what time did the robbery take place? ........................................
10. Where did the robbers lock the employees? ........................................

¡Vamos a escuchar! 1

**11.** What exactly was stolen? ..................................................................

**12.** The robbers escaped:

    (a)  in an old car.

    (b)  in a red car.

    (c)  on an old motorbike.

    (d)  on a red motorbike.

    Write the correct letter in the box. ☐

**13.** Why do the police feel confident about catching the thieves?

..................................................................................................

\* \* \*

🔘 88

**14.** Who is on strike? ..................................................................

**15.** How long is the strike reckoned to last? ..................................

**16.** What incident took place yesterday? ..........................................

..................................................................................................

¡Vamos a escuchar! 1

# 43. Mi piso

**Marisol describes the apartment she lives in.**

🔊 89

1. Marisol lives in the centre of the city.     True ☐     False ☐

2. Is the area where Marisol lives noisy?     Yes ☐     No ☐

3. This is the fifth apartment she has lived in.     True ☐     False ☐

4. How many are in her family? ....................................................

5. What rooms does the apartment contain? ........................................
...................................................................................

6. In good weather, what does her mother put on the balcony?
...................................................................................

7. Which of the following items (besides a bed) are in Marisol's bedroom? Tick the correct boxes:

|  |  |  |
|---|---|---|
| table ☐ | chair ☐ | wardrobe ☐ |
| lamp ☐ | computer ☐ | posters ☐ |
| mirror ☐ | DVDs ☐ | books ☐ |
| photos ☐ | TV ☐ | calendar ☐ |

8. What colour are the walls and curtains of her bedroom? ..................

9. Her bedroom is:     big ☐     small ☐

¡Vamos a escuchar! 1

# 44. Mensajes telefónicos (1)

**You will hear three telephone messages. Listen to them and answer the questions.**

🔘 90

1. Where has Luci just arrived? ............................................................
2. With which family relation is she staying? .............................................
3. What tourist sights is the relative going to show Luci? ..............................
   ...................................................................................
4. When is Luci going to telephone her mother again? ...................................

✳ ✳ ✳

🔘 91

5. How long has this young man been waiting for his girlfriend? .......................
6. What time is it? ...................................................................
7. When is the film starting? .........................................................

✳ ✳ ✳

🔘 92

8. When exactly is la Sra. Pérez's appointment with the dentist?
   ...................................................................................
9. Why does the receptionist ask her to phone the dental clinic?
   ...................................................................................
10. What is the phone number of the dental clinic? ....................................

¡Vamos a escuchar! 1

## 45. Reservando un billete de avión

La Sra. Pujol telephones a travel agency to book a return flight to Barcelona.

🔘 93

1. On what date does la Sra. Pujol wish to travel to Barcelona? ……………………
2. On what date does she intend to return? ……………………………………
3. What is the first departure and arrival time she is offered?

    departing Madrid ………………… arriving Barcelona …………………………
4. Why does she reject this flight? ………………………………………………
5. What is the next departure and arrival time she is offered?

    departing Madrid ………………… arriving Barcelona …………………………
6. Her flight will arrive back in Madrid at 10.15 p.m.   True ❏   False ❏
7. How much will the return flight cost? ……………………………………
8. What is her Visa credit card number? ……………………………………
9. In what month does her Visa card expire? ……………………………………
10. When is she going to pick up her ticket from the travel agency?

    ……………………………………………………………………………

¡Vamos a escuchar! 1

## 46. ¿Dónde está?

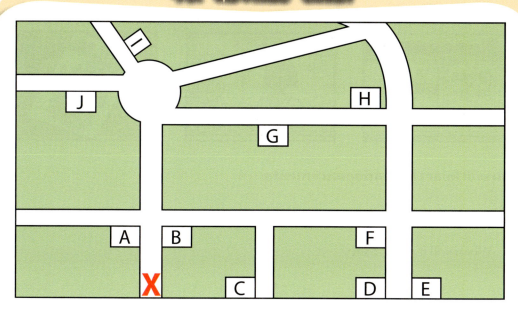

**You will hear three people asking for directions.**

🔴 2–4

In each case, 'X' marks the spot where the speakers are. Write down the letter which corresponds to: (1) the position of the tourist office, (2) the Ye-yé disco and (3) the town hall.

1. The tourist office is letter ☐

2. The Ye-yé disco is letter ☐

3. The town hall is letter ☐

¡Vamos a escuchar! 1

# 47. Anuncios (2)

**You will hear three announcements.**

◉ 5

1. Why is this supermarket closed? ....................................................
2. When will it open again? ..........................................................

✱ ✱ ✱

◉ 6

3. On what date is Mother's Day? ....................................................
4. The shop gives customers six ideas for a present which they can buy for Mother's Day. What are they?

   (i) ........................ (ii) ........................ (iii) ........................

   (iv) ........................ (v) ........................ (vi) ........................

5. The shop also suggests that customers can buy a voucher instead. For what value can vouchers be bought?

   (i) ................................ (ii) ................................

   (iii) ................................ (iv) ................................

✱ ✱ ✱

◉ 7

6. On what basis will Clarins offer customers a free beauty treatment?
   ..........................................................................
7. Until when is the offer valid? ....................................................

¡Vamos a escuchar! 1

# 48. Una entrevista con un actor famoso

**A famous actor, Nacho Beltrán, is interviewed on a radio programme.**

🔴 8

1. The listeners: (a) phone in with a question or (b) send a question by text message.

   Write the correct letter in the box.

2. Fill in the information according to what Nacho says:

| Favourite colour | |
| --- | --- |
| Favourite food | |
| Best quality | |
| Worst defect | |
| Favourite animal | |
| Person he loves most | |
| Favourite place | |
| Pastimes | |
| Professional ambitions | |
| Personal hopes | |
| His ideal partner would be … | |

¡Vamos a escuchar! 1

# 49. ¿Qué país es?

**You will hear some brief details about four countries. Can you guess what the four countries are?**

🔴 9–12

    (i) ……………………………………… (ii) ………………………………………………

    (iii) ……………………………………… (iv) ………………………………………………

Now listen again, and supply details regarding each country, according to the information you hear.

    (i) ………………………………………………………………………………………………
    ………………………………………………………………………………………………

    (ii) ………………………………………………………………………………………………
    ………………………………………………………………………………………………

    (iii) ………………………………………………………………………………………………
    ………………………………………………………………………………………………

    (iv) ………………………………………………………………………………………………
    ………………………………………………………………………………………………

¡Vamos a escuchar! 1

## 50. La Sra. Guzmán se encuentra mal

**El Sr. Guzmán has taken the morning off work to help his sick wife.**

🔴 13

1. What is the first thing el Sr. Guzmán must do?

   ..................................................................................................................

2. His wife asks him to do three jobs at home. What are they?

   (i) ............................................................................................................

   (ii) ...........................................................................................................

   (iii) ..........................................................................................................

3. She asks him to buy six items in the supermarket. What are they?

   (i) ........................... (ii) ........................... (iii) ...........................

   (iv) ........................... (v) ........................... (vi) ...........................

4. What does la Sra. Guzmán ask her husband to buy her on the way home?

   ..................................................................................................................

## 51. ¡Vaya récord!

**You will hear details of some record-breaking activities.**

1. How many T-shirts did this DJ put on at the one time? .....................................
2. How long did it take him to put the T-shirts on? .....................................
3. How many kilos more did the DJ weigh when he had finished putting on the T-shirts? .....................................
4. What picture was on the last T-shirt? .....................................

*  *  *

5. Fill in the ingredients of this record-breaking paella.

¡Vamos a escuchar! 1

| QUANTITY | INGREDIENT |
|---|---|
| 1100 litres | |
| | paprika |
| | |
| | |
| | chicken and rabbit |
| | |
| | food colouring |
| | |
| 13,000 litres | |

6. How many cooks were involved in the preparation of this paella? ................

7. At what time did the cooks start preparing the paella? ............................

8. How many hours did they take to prepare it? ........................................

* * *

○ 16

9. In what city was this record broken? ..................................................

10. What was the weather like that day? .................................................

11. The event took place in a city centre car park.     True ☐     False ☐

12. What was the average age of the participants? ...................................

13. What record did they break? ...........................................................

14. How many people took part? ...........................................................

15. What were they wearing? ................................................................

16. Where is their Guinness world record certificate kept?

..........................................................................................................

¡Vamos a escuchar! 1

## 52. El tiempo en Galicia

**You will hear a weather forecast. Listen carefully and answer the questions below.**

🔴 17

1. Skies will be:      generally clear ☐      cloudy ☐
2. Showers will be:     light ☐      heavy ☐
3. Where will it be stormy? ...................................................................
4. Where will it be foggy? ....................................................................
5. From what direction will the wind blow? ................................................
6. Temperatures will be:
    (a) a maximum of ....................... degrees and
    (b) a minimum of ....................... degrees.

¡Vamos a escuchar! 1

# 53. Ayudando en casa

**Various members of the Sánchez family describe how they help in the house.**

🔴 18

1. The grandmother says her daughter is sick in hospital.   True ☐    False ☐
2. What does the grandmother do every day? ...........................................
   ................................................................................................
3. What does she do at the weekend? ..................................................
4. In what way does she help out with the grandchildren? ............................
   ................................................................................................

∗ ∗ ∗

🔴 19

5. Where does Paco help out most? ....................................................
6. What four things does he do? ........................................................
   ................................................................................................

∗ ∗ ∗

## ¡Vamos a escuchar! 1

🔴 20

**7.** Why does the father not help out a lot?

..................................................................................................................

**8.** To which two places does he take his children occasionally?

(i) ....................................... (ii) .......................................

**9.** In what two ways does he help out in the house?

(i) ....................................... (ii) .......................................

* * *

🔴 21

**10.** In what three ways does Nuria help out?

(i) ....................................... (ii) .......................................

(iii) .......................................

¡Vamos a escuchar! 1

# 54. ¿En qué puedo ayudarle?

You will hear four short conversations. Listen carefully and answer the questions below.

🔴 22
1. What is the person buying? ..................................................................
2. What is just opposite the speakers? ........................................................

\* \* \*

🔴 23
3. Where do you think these people are? .....................................................
4. The man is given information on ..........................................................
   ..........................................................................................

\* \* \*

🔴 24
5. What symptoms does the man describe to the doctor? .......................................
   ..........................................................................................
6. What does the doctor advise him to do? ...................................................
   ..........................................................................................
7. What does the doctor prefer not to do? ...................................................
8. What does she say he should do if he starts to feel worse? ...............................
   ..........................................................................................

\* \* \*

🔴 25
9. What is this girl looking for? ...........................................................
10. Where is it? ............................................................................

¡Vamos a escuchar! 1

## 55. ¿A qué se dedica?

**You will hear four people talking about their job.**

🔴 26

1. What is this person's job? ......................................................
2. What must he do? ...........................................................
3. When does he get extra money?

   ..................................................................................
4. What exactly must he wear when he is working? ...................................

   ..................................................................................
5. What aspect of his job does he not like? .......................................

\* \* \*

🔴 27

6. This person is:

   a vet ☐    a farmer's wife ☐    a zookeeper ☐    an animal breeder ☐

   Tick the correct box.

## ¡Vamos a escuchar! 1

7. Why does she like her job? .................................................
8. What disadvantage does this job have?
   .................................................................................

*  *  *

🔴 28

9. What is this person's job? .................................................
10. Why does he not like it? .................................................
11. When he has to go somewhere on his day off, how does he get there?

    He ........................... or else he ...........................

*  *  *

🔴 29

12. How exactly does this woman spend her day? ...........................
    .................................................................................

13. At times she feels:   tired ☐   annoyed ☐   bored ☐

    Tick the correct box.

14. This woman thinks it is important to ...........................
    .................................................................................

¡Vamos a escuchar! 1

# 56. En una boutique

**A woman goes shopping for something nice to wear.**

🔴 30

1. When is this woman's daughter getting married? ...........................
2. In what price range is she thinking of buying a suit? ...........................
3. What colours would she not consider for her outfit? ...........................
   ...........................
4. What colours would she consider? ...........................
   ...........................
5. What size is she? ...........................
6. How does the shop assistant describe the Carolina Herrera suit which she shows to the customer? ...........................
7. Where is the fitting room? ...........................
8. Describe the blouse that the assistant invites the woman to try on.
   ...........................
9. What is the total price of the jacket and skirt? ...........................
10. How much is the blouse? ...........................
11. What does the woman think her husband's reaction will be to the purchase?
    ...........................

¡Vamos a escuchar! 1

# 57. Mensajes telefónicos (2)

**You will hear three telephone messages**.

🔴 31

1. Why is Rosa cancelling her date with her boyfriend? ...............................
   ..................................................................................
2. Where were they planning to go? ................................................
3. What is the only thing she wants to do? .......................................
4. When will she ring her boyfriend? ..............................................

\* \* \*

🔴 32

5. Where is Teo phoning from? ....................................................
6. At what time is the football match starting? .................................
7. Where does he intend to watch it? .............................................
8. What is his phone number? .....................................................

\* \* \*

🔴 33

9. What are the girl's plans for the evening? ....................................
   ..................................................................................
10. At what time will she return home? ..........................................
11. How will she get home? ........................................................

¡Vamos a escuchar! 1

# 58. Juana visita a una adivina

**Juana describes a visit to a fortune-teller.**

🔴 34

1. When did Juana go to the fortune-teller? ................................................
2. What was she told regarding her examinations?
   ................................................................................................
3. What sort of person would she marry? ................................................
4. Where would they live? ................................................................
5. How many children would they have? ................................................

6. They would always be happy.              True ☐        False ☐
7. They would have occasional health problems.   True ☐        False ☐
8. What kind of problem would she have in the near future?
   ................................................................................................
9. In what way was the fortune-teller correct? ................................................
   ................................................................................................

¡Vamos a escuchar! 1

# 59. Una estudiante nueva

A new student has just arrived and chats to a classmate before class begins.

🔴 35

1. Why did Rosario's family move to Granada? .................................................
2. Where did they live previously? ...............................................................
3. When did she arrive in Granada? ..............................................................
4. Juan says his school is:

   (a)  fantastic.         (b)  very good.

   (c)  not bad.           (d)  not great.

   Write the correct letter in the box. ☐

5. Which two teachers does he single out as being nice?

   (i) ................................... (ii) ...........................................
6. Which teacher does he think is awful? ......................................................
7. On what days do the pupils have homework? ...............................................
8. What sports are played? .......................................................................
9. At what time is there an inter-schools match that evening? ...........................
10. What does Juan say he will do? ..............................................................

¡Vamos a escuchar! 1

# 60. En una agencia de viajes

**Merche**, a receptionist in the Buen Viaje travel agency, takes three telephone calls.

🔴 36

1. What exactly has been cancelled? ........................................................
2. What is the reason for the cancellation? ...............................................
3. Why would the travel agent need to know? ...........................................

\* \* \*

🔴 37

4. Who is the second caller? ..................................................................
5. What bad news does she wish to convey? ............................................
   ........................................................................................................

\* \* \*

🔴 38

6. What does this caller wish to do? .......................................................
7. What establishment did he think he was telephoning? ...........................

¡Vamos a escuchar! 1

# 61. El gazpacho andaluz

**You will hear some information about a popular Spanish dish.**

🔴 39

1. Gazpacho is: (a) a salad dish (b) a casserole dish (c) a soup

   Write the correct letter in the box. ☐

2. When is it most enjoyed? ....................................................

3. For how many people is the recipe designed?

   ....................................................

4. Supply the missing information in the grid.

| QUANTITY | INGREDIENT |
|---|---|
|  | cucumber |
|  |  |
|  |  |
|  |  |
|  |  |
|  |  |
| 1/10 litre |  |

5. In what way does the preparation differ nowadays from the way gazpacho was prepared before? ....................................................

....................................................

¡Vamos a escuchar! 1

## 62. En un pequeño hotel

**La Sra. Ibáñez runs a small hotel and is speaking to a guest who has just arrived in the city.**

🔴 40

1. What aspect of the dinner does the visitor particularly compliment?
   ..................................................................................................
2. What reason does la Sra. Ibáñez give for its quality?
   ..................................................................................................
3. What three places does she recommend that the visitor see?
   (i).................................................(ii)................................................
   (iii) ........................................
4. Where, in relation to the town, is the last place she mentions?
   ..................................................................................................
5. How can the visitor get there? ...................................................
6. She suggests two places where he can go to relax. What are they?
   (i) ................................................(ii) ...............................................
7. Where is the tourist office situated? ...............................................
8. When is he going to the tourist office? ...........................................

¡Vamos a escuchar! 1

# 63. Mi día ideal

**A housewife describes her idea of a perfect day.**

🔴 41

1. How many children does this woman have? ...........................................
2. What might her husband do with the children to give her a rest?
   ...........................................................................................
3. What would she do before going out, on a day like this? ...........................
   ...........................................................................................
4. On leaving home, where would she go first? .........................................
5. Where would she eat, and with whom? ...............................................
6. What sort of shop would she: (i) visit; (ii) not visit?
   (i) ........................................... (ii) ...........................................
7. What does she have little opportunity to do when the family are at home?
   ...........................................................................................

¡Vamos a escuchar! 1

# 64. En el restaurante

**A couple are ordering a meal in a restaurant.**

🔴 42

1. Fill in the grid.

|  | THE MAN ORDERS | THE WOMAN ORDERS |
|---|---|---|
| First course |  |  |
| Second course |  |  |

2. Apart from ice-cream, what choices are available for the third course?

   (i) ……………………… (ii) ……………………… (iii) ………………………

3. What flavours of ice-cream does the waiter offer? ………………………………

   (i) …………………………………… (ii) ……………………………………

   (iii) …………………………………… (iv) ……………………………………

4. The man orders a bottle of sweet white wine.    True ☐    False ☐

5. What does the man discover? ………………………………………………

¡Vamos a escuchar! 1

## 65. En el aeropuerto de Dublín

**Two friends returning to Spain meet by chance in Dublin airport, and tell of their experiences in Ireland.**

🔴 43

1. How long was Pedro in Dublin? ......................................................
2. Pedro was:

    (a) on an exchange.     (b) at a summer camp.     (c) on a sporting holiday.

    Write the correct letter in the box. ☐

3. What three activities did Pedro enjoy, during his stay in Ireland?

    (i) .......................... (ii) .......................... (iii) ..........................

4. With whom did he practise his English? ..........................................
5. How long was Mari Carmen in Ireland? ..........................................
6. She was a paying guest with a family.      True ☐      False ☐
7. Mari Carmen attended an English course because:

    (a) she found it difficult to take notes in English.

    (b) her exam results in English were poor.

    (c) her parents thought she might enjoy an English course in Ireland.

    Write the correct letter in the box. ☐

8. What did she think of Irish food? ..................................................
9. Why did her English not improve much? ..........................................

¡Vamos a escuchar! 1

# 66. Por favor, ¿para ir a ...?

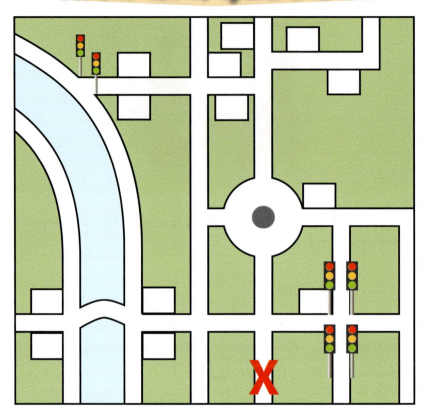

**Three people are lost.**

🔴 44–46

Write A, B and C in the correct boxes, to indicate the position of: (a) the Imperial cinema, (b) the pharmacy and (c) the Acuario restaurant. In each case, 'X' marks the position of the speakers.

¡Vamos a escuchar! 1

# 67. Número equivocado

**Juan dials the wrong number.**

🔴 47

1. What comment did Juan make to his girlfriend yesterday? ..........................
   ...................................................................................................................
2. What number did he dial by mistake? ..................................................
3. Why did he think he was talking to his girlfriend? ...................................
   ...................................................................................................................
4. What does the caller think his girlfriend should do? ..............................
   ...................................................................................................................

¡Vamos a escuchar! 1

## 68. Juan tiene gripe

**Juan feels unwell and the doctor has come to visit him.**

🔴 48

1. Tick which symptoms Juan describes:

   | He is thirsty. ☐ | He feels hot and cold. ☐ |
   |---|---|
   | He has a blocked nose. ☐ | He has lost his appetite. ☐ |
   | He is sleeping a lot. ☐ | He finds it difficult to swallow. ☐ |
   | He feels weak. ☐ | He has a headache. ☐ |
   | He has an earache. ☐ | He has a cough. ☐ |

2. When did he start to feel unwell? ..................................................

3. How long must he stay in bed? ..................................................

4. He must use a hot water bottle.    True ☐    False ☐

5. What instructions is he given regarding the antibiotic? .......................
   ..................................................

6. What does the doctor advise: (i) if he feels worse and (ii) if he feels better?
   (i) .................................... (ii) ....................................

7. What consolation does she offer him? ..................................................

¡Vamos a escuchar! 1

# 69. Anuncios (3)

You will hear three announcements. Listen carefully and answer the questions.

🔴 49

1. What establishment is offering a discount? ...........................................
2. On what day does the discount apply? ..............................................
3. Until when does the offer run? .....................................................
4. What percentage discount is offered? ..............................................
5. Who is entitled to avail of the offer? ...............................................

\* \* \*

🔴 50

6. What item has been found? ........................................................
7. The item was discovered in a department store.   True ☐      False ☐
8. Where can the item be collected? ..................................................
9. On what conditions can it be collected? ...........................................
   ......................................................................................

\* \* \*

🔴 51

10. What means of transport are these travellers to Ceuta using? .....................
11. At what time are they: (a) departing and (b) returning?

    (a) ........................................... (b) ...........................................

¡Vamos a escuchar! 1

## 70. YouTube

You will hear some information about the highly successful website YouTube.

🔴 52

1. How many friends were involved in starting up the YouTube website? ...........
2. What did the friends initially use as their office? ........................................
3. When was the YouTube website activated? ..............................................
4. When did Google buy the website? ........................................................
5. How much did Google pay for the website? .............................................
6. Approximately how many clips are viewed daily? ....................................
7. What examples are given of the types of video clips that are put on the website?

   (i) ........................ (ii) ............................ (iii) ............................

   (iv) ........................(v) ........................ (vi) ............................

8. Which of the following languages are mentioned as featuring in YouTube video clips? Tick the correct boxes.

   Russian ☐   Portuguese ☐   French ☐   Swedish ☐   German ☐

   Spanish ☐   English ☐   Italian ☐   Irish ☐   Chinese ☐

¡Vamos a escuchar! 1

## 71. En la oficina del Jefe de Estudios

**Carmen's family have just moved to a new area, and Carmen is speaking to the Head of Studies on her first day in the new school.**

🔴 53

1. What is Carmen's surname? ......................................................
2. What age is she? ....................................................................
3. What date is her birthday? .......................................................
4. What subjects was Carmen studying in her previous school? .........
   ..............................................................................................
5. What does she consider to be her best subjects? .......................
6. What subject does she find difficult? ........................................
7. What consolation does the Head of Studies offer her in this respect?
   ..............................................................................................
8. She is beginning school the same day.     True ☐     False ☐

¡Vamos a escuchar! 1

## 72. Guía del Ocio

**You will hear about a very useful little magazine called *Guía del Ocio*, which is published in Spain.**

🔴 54

1. Approximately how many pages does this magazine contain? ....................
2. On what day of the week does it appear? ............................................
3. Approximately how many cities does it cover? ....................................
4. The magazine includes information on:

   (i) ....................................... (ii) .......................................

   (iii) ....................................... (iv) .......................................

   (v) ....................................... (vi) .......................................

   (vii) ....................................... (viii) .......................................

5. The magazine is quite expensive.   True ☐    False ☐

6. What information does the front page typically include?

   ................................................................................................

7. For whom is the magazine particularly useful?

   ................................................................................................

¡Vamos a escuchar! 1

# 73. Una visita a Madrid: sábado

**Juan spent a weekend with his aunt in Madrid. Listen to what they did on Saturday.**

🍊 55

1. In what part of Madrid is the Puerta del Sol? ..................................................
2. On what occasion in particular do a lot of people go to the Puerta del Sol?
   ..................................................................................................................
3. What is a plaque on the ground in this square believed to indicate?
   ..................................................................................................................
4. What refreshments did Juan and his aunt have? ..................................
   ..................................................................................................................
5. What three places did they visit around the Plaza de Oriente?
   ..................................................................................................................
6. What number bus did they take to go to the Zoo and Aquarium? ................
7. How many litres of water are used in the Aquarium? ..............................
8. What did Juan and his aunt have for their evening meal?
   ..................................................................................................................

¡Vamos a escuchar! 1

## 74. Una visita a Madrid: domingo

**Juan describes how he and his aunt spent Sunday.**

🔴 56

1. Juan bought the following presents in the Rastro flea market:

| For his aunt    |  |
|-----------------|--|
| For his mother  |  |
| For his brother |  |
| For his father  |  |
| For himself     |  |

2. What did Juan's aunt buy for him? .................................................................

3. What was the score in the football match between Real Madrid and Barça?
   ........................................................................................................................

4. From what year does the Botín restaurant date? ............................................

5. What did Juan and his aunt have to eat in the restaurant?
   ........................................................................................................................

6. How did they get home? ................................................................................

¡Vamos a escuchar! 1

## 75. Un padre llama a su hija a Irlanda

**María's parents are planning to visit their daughter shortly in Ireland. María's father phones her from Spain.**

🔴 57

1. On what day are María's parents arriving? ...........................................
2. What is the flight number? ...................................................................
3. At what time will the flight arrive? ......................................................
4. What is the first thing María asks her father to bring over? ......................
   ...........................................................................................................
5. What kinds of DVDs would she like? ...................................................
6. What food does she ask for? Tick the correct box.

   olives ☐     peppers ☐     anchovies ☐

7. Why would she like her father to bring over a flag of Spain?
   ...........................................................................................................

87

¡Vamos a escuchar! 1

# 76. Noticias (2)

**You will hear three news items.**

🔴 58

1. What did the police discover hidden in the apartment of this man?

   .................................................................................................

2. Give details of the other people arrested in the operation.

   .................................................................................................

* * *

🔴 59

3. How many people died in traffic accidents during Holy Week? ....................

4. How many were injured? ........................................................................

5. What did the Traffic Authorities say the main reasons for traffic accidents were?

   (i) ........................................... (ii) ...........................................
   
   (iii) ......................................... (iv) ...........................................
   
   (v) ...........................................

* * *

🔴 60

6. When did this parrot escape? ...............................................................

7. Why did the owner of the parrot open the bird-cage? ...............................

8. How did the vet know where to find the owner of the parrot?

   .................................................................................................

¡Vamos a escuchar! 1

# 77. Un turista busca información

A tourist has just arrived in town and goes to the tourist office for some information.

🔴 61

1. Where is the tourist office in relation to the cathedral?

   ..................................................................................................................

2. What three tourist sights does the woman suggest the tourist visit?

   ..................................................................................................................

3. What is the restaurant Frutos del Mar famous for?

   ..................................................................................................................

4. In what area of the city is Frutos del Mar? ...........................................

   ..................................................................................................................

5. What is the number of the bus that goes there? ...................................

6. The woman looks up the phone number:

   (a) on the computer.    (b) in the yellow pages.    (c) in a notebook.

   Write the correct letter in the box. ☐

7. What is the phone number of Frutos del Mar? ...................................

8. Where is the Banco de España, in relation to the tourist office?

   ..................................................................................................................

¡Vamos a escuchar! 1

# 78. Pastel de chocolate

**You will hear a recipe for a delicious chocolate dessert.**

 62

1. For this chocolate dessert you will need:

| QUANTITY | INGREDIENT |
|---|---|
|  |  |
|  | butter |
| 4 large spoons |  |
|  |  |
|  |  |

2. What two ingredients are mixed first? ...................................................
3. For how long should the dessert be left in the oven? ...............................
4. At what temperature should the oven be set? .......................................
5. What could be served with the dessert? ..............................................

¡Vamos a escuchar! 1

# 79. Anuncios (4)

**You will hear three announcements. Listen carefully and answer the questions below.**

🔴 63

1. At what time will the bus from Avila arrive? ........................................
2. Why exactly is it delayed? ...............................................................
   ...................................................................................................

* * *

🔴 64

3. What age is Pablo? .........................................................................
4. What is his hair like? ......................................................................
5. Describe his clothes. ......................................................................
6. Where should he be brought if he is found? ......................................

* * *

🔴 65

7. This boutique is selling off the last of its stock.    True ☐    False ☐
8. Where is the boutique situated? ......................................................
9. What are its opening and closing hours? .........................................
10. Is it open every day?                              Yes ☐    No ☐

¡Vamos a escuchar! 1

## 80. Algunas estadísticas sobre Las Fallas

You will hear some approximate statistics regarding the Fallas festival in Valencia which culminates with the burning of hundreds of Fallas effigies in the streets. Fill in the missing information.

🔴 66

| | |
|---|---|
| Number of Fallas seen in the streets | |
| Number of firemen used during the festival | |
| Amount of water used by the the firemen | |
| Amount of money spent by the revellers | € |
| Number of hours' sleep the revellers get nightly | |
| Amount of rubbish accumulated | |
| Cost of damages | € |
| Number of people employed to clean the streets | |
| Number of calls made to the emergency services | |
| Number of people attended by the Red Cross | |

¡Vamos a escuchar! 1

## 81. Un albergue para jóvenes

**Two friends book into a youth hostel.**
🔴 67
1. How many nights do the girls want to stay? ..............................................
2. What does the woman in charge ask them to give her? ............................
3. By what time must they be back at night? ................................................
4. At what time are the lights put out? .........................................................
5. The woman mentions two ways the visitors must help. What are they?
   (i)....................................... (ii).......................................
6. Give details of the foreign visitors staying. ...............................................
   ........................................................................................

¡Vamos a escuchar! 1

## 82. Manolito quiere más dinero

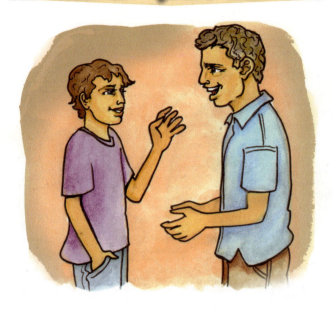

**Manolito talks to his father about getting a part-time job.**

🔴 68

1. On what day does Manolito suggest he could work? ...................................
2. What does he spend his money on?
   (i) ........................ (ii) ........................... (iii) ...........................
   (iv) ........................... (v) ............................
3. What kind of job does Manolito's father object to his son doing and why?
   ...................................................................................................
4. What two comments does his father make about working in a shop?
   ...................................................................................................
5. Where is Manolito going this summer and why?
   ...................................................................................................
6. What reason does Manolito's father give when he agrees to Manolito taking on a part-time job?
   ...................................................................................................

¡Vamos a escuchar! 1

## 83. Una mañana catastrófica

**Juana recounts a bad experience**.

🔴 69

1. What age is Juana? ..................................................................
2. Where does she work? ..............................................................
3. At what time does the office open? ...........................................
4. What is her boss like? ..............................................................
5. The shower didn't work that morning.   True ☐   False ☐
6. She only had time for a quick breakfast.   True ☐   False ☐
7. On what floor does Juana live? .................................................
8. What was the weather like that morning? .................................
9. How long did she wait for the bus? ...........................................
10. How did she get to work? ........................................................
11. Why was the office closed? ......................................................

95

¡Vamos a escuchar! 1

# 84. Problemas

**Javier rings his girlfriend.**

🔴 70

1. Why can Conchi not see Javier so frequently? ............................................
   ............................................................................................

2. When is the only time she can see him? ....................................................
   ............................................................................................

3. Where and at what time do they plan to meet? ............................................
   ............................................................................................

4. What do they plan to do? ....................................................................
   ............................................................................................

¡Vamos a escuchar! 1

# 85. Noticias (3)

**You will hear some news items and the results of the Lottery.**

🔴 71

1. How many taxi drivers took part in this protest? ....................................
2. What were they protesting about? ....................................
3. What form did their protest take? ....................................
   ....................................
4. How did their protest affect other people? ....................................
   ....................................

\* \* \*

🔴 72

5. What two countries were playing in this football match? ....................................
   ....................................
6. What was the final score? ....................................
7. How many hooligans were involved in disturbances after the match? ....................................
8. What did they throw at the police? ....................................
9. How many police were injured? ....................................
10. Approximately how many hooligans were arrested? ....................................

\* \* \*

🔴 73

11. What were today's Lottery numbers? ....................................
12. The Lottery is now worth .................................... euros.

¡Vamos a escuchar! 1

## 86. El tiempo para esta semana

**You will hear a short weather forecast**.

🔴 74

1. What will the weather be like early in the week? ………………………………………

2. There will be:

   storms ☐        in the northeast ☐       on Tuesday ☐

   flooding ☐      in the northwest ☐       on Wednesday ☐

   Tick where appropriate.

3. From Thursday it will be:

   misty ☐

   cloudy ☐    in the north.

   foggy ☐

   Tick where appropriate.

¡Vamos a escuchar! 1

4. What will the maximum and minimum temperatures in the north be later in the week?

   maximum ............................ minimum ..................................

5. What will the weather in the south be like? .........................................

6. What will the maximum and minimum temperatures be in the south?

   maximum ............................ minimum ..................................

¡Vamos a escuchar! 1

# 87. La Navidad se acerca

Carlos and his sister Juana are discussing the Christmas presents they want to buy members of the family.

🔴 75

1. What date is it today? ....................................................................
2. What do Carlos and Juana decide to buy their mother? ..............................
3. What does Juana suggest they buy their father? ....................................
4. Why does Carlos reject this suggestion? ...........................................
   ....................................................................................
5. What does he suggest instead? .....................................................
6. How can this present be of benefit to Carlos and his sister? .....................
   ....................................................................................
7. What do they decide **not** to buy their grandfather? .............................
8. What reason do they have for this decision? ......................................
   ....................................................................................
9. They decide to buy him pyjamas instead.   True ☐      False ☐
10. What will they buy their younger brother? .......................................
11. When do they decide to go shopping? .............................................

¡Vamos a escuchar! 1

# 88. Los Sanfermines

**You will hear information about a week of festivities that take place in Pamplona every year.**

🔴 76

1. Pamplona is situated in the   north ☐   south ☐   east ☐   west ☐   of Spain.

2. Between what dates do these festivities take place? ................................

3. At what time do the festivities start? ..................................................

4. At what time do they end on the last night? ........................................

5. Where do tourists come from? ..........................................................

6. At what time does the 'running of the bulls' start each morning? ..................

7. For approximately how many minutes do the bulls run?

   three minutes ☐    thirteen minutes ☐    thirty minutes ☐

8. How many metres do they run? ........................................................

## ¡Vamos a escuchar! 1

9. Where do they run to? ...............................................................

10. Describe the clothes which many youths and men wear during the week.

    ...............................................................

11. Apart from the obvious danger, why is it particularly dangerous for certain people to run along with the bulls? ...............................................................

    ...............................................................

12. What other activities take place during the festivities?

    (i) ........................ (ii) ........................ (iii) ........................

13. The celebrations finish with (a) a prayer (b) a fire cracker (c) a song.

    Put the correct letter in the box ☐

¡Vamos a escuchar! 1

## 89. Lidia pierde una bolsa

**Lidia goes to the Enquiries desk of a department store to ask about a shopping bag she has left somewhere in the store.**

🔴 77

1. What does the shopping bag contain? ...............................................
   ...................................................................................................

2. On what floor did she buy the items which were in the shopping bag?
   ...................................................................................................

3. What did she buy on the first floor? .................................................
   ...................................................................................................

4. What did she buy on the fifth floor? .................................................

5. On what floor did she buy a pair of shoes? .....................................

6. What does the woman at the Enquiries desk suggest that Lidia do?
   ...................................................................................................

¡Vamos a escuchar! 1

# 90. En la clase

**A teacher's patience is tried!**

🔴 78

1. What time is it when Isabel arrives in class? ..............................................
2. What bus did she catch by mistake? ..................................................
3. What advice does her teacher give her? ..............................................
4. What subject is he teaching? ..........................................................
5. Where did Alejandro go yesterday? ...................................................
6. How did this affect his homework? ...................................................
7. What advice does the teacher give him? ..............................................